New York City 10/12/18

Beauty beyond Reason

For Joe & Lynn,
& for glorious dance.

Also by Garrett Buhl Robinson

Martha, a poem
flowing stone, poems
Möbius Sphere, poems
Broken Open, poems
Fortune, poems and libretti

Zoë, a novella
Nunatak, a novel

www.gbrobinson.com

Beauty beyond Reason

songs for dance

Garrett Buhl Robinson

Dendritic Path Press
The path I take is the path I create.

copyright by Garrett Buhl Robinson
© 1998, 2002, 2013, 2014, 2015, 2017 & 2018
All Rights Reserved

Beauty beyond Reason

Prologue	3
Upon the Highest Peak	7
A Lifetime Every Day	9
To Touch Eternity	13
Answer	15
Some Say	17
Relying on Rivals, Competing against Friends	20
The Noble Part	23
Absolutely Endless	26
Partnering the Heart	30
Epilogue	33

Pas Seul

Serenade	37
Pas Seul	39
Exchanging Gifts	41
The Way You Say	43
Poured from a Performance	45
Dancing Elms	47
Agape	49

for the Dancers

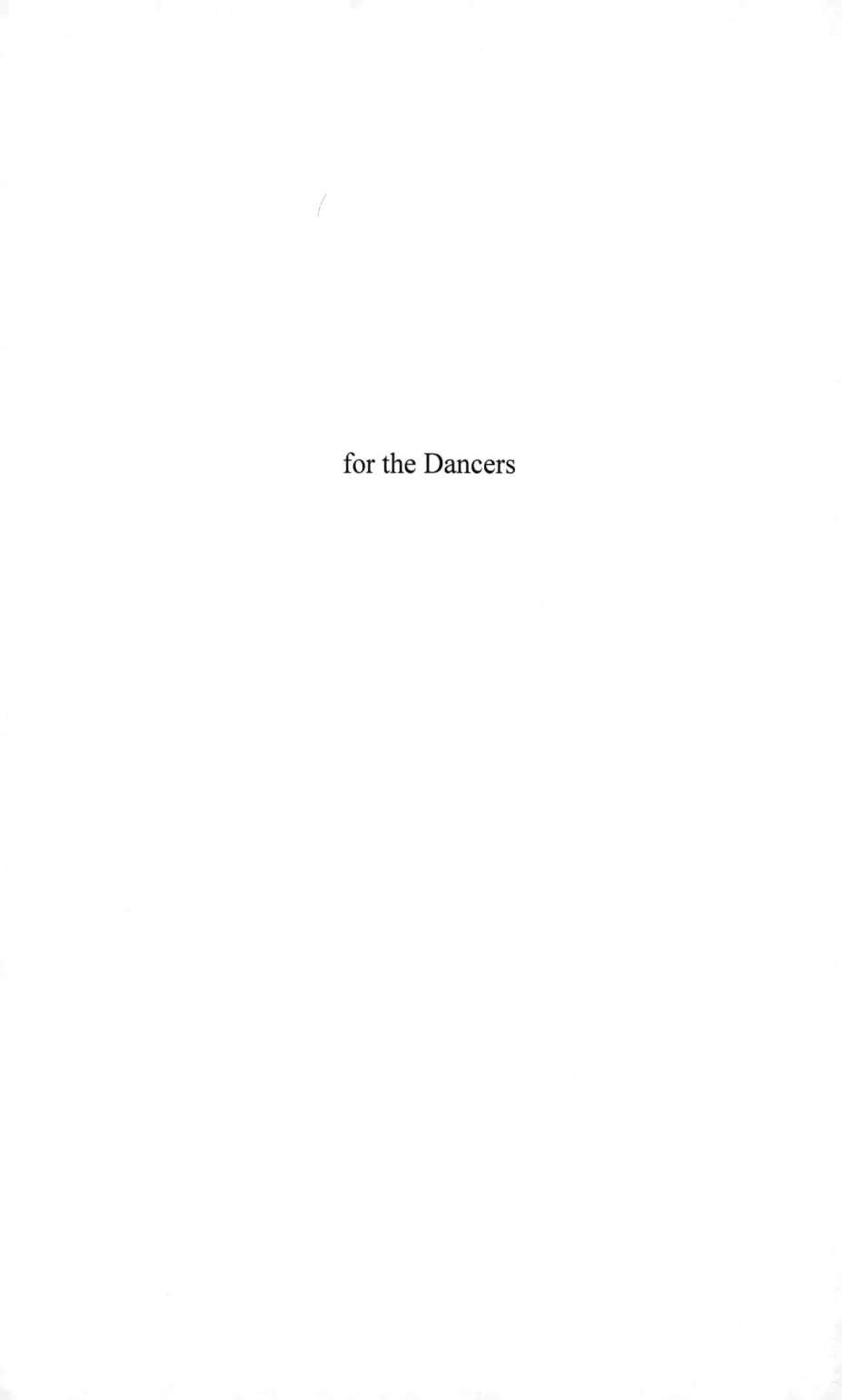

Beauty beyond Reason

a libretto
for a ballet chanté

Cast
A Dancer
An Ensemble of Dancers
A Poet

Prologue
– for Edwin Denby

Many have asked me how
   I was drawn to the art,
when did I discover dance,
   where did my devotion start?

Did I know a dancer?
   Did I fall in love?
Was it a particular night
   or a light from above?

Did it make me feel elite
   with sophisticated tastes?
Was it a whimsical fancy
   or was it my fate?

Was it part of a class,
   did I go with a group?
Was it something forced on me
   while I was in school?

Was it just a measure
   of an arbitrary rule?
Or just something
   I was expected to do?

Was it the passion,
   was it the release,

was it the one thing in the world
   that could set me free?

Was it the solemn work
   and the cloistered life?
Was there something about it
   that felt divine?

Was it the movement?
   Was it the music?
Was it the rapture?
   Was it the beauty?

I did my best to answer
   though it is difficult to say
what is far beyond words
   and impossible to explain –

It is softer than water,
   yet harder than steel,
flowing smooth as a river,
   yet running uphill.

My devotion is without doubt
   and I am always convinced
every performance night
   at every show I attend.

BEAUTY BEYOND REASON

It is the struggle of love,
   the embodiment of freedom.
It is the passion for life –
   beauty beyond reason.

Upon the Highest Peak
– for TR

POET

On a mountain rising up from the deep,
set to bound the length of eternity,
she stands on point at the breathtaking peak.

The distant springs pour forth the purest streams,
confluences drawing from centuries
that flow into rivers to fill the sea.

From the fathomless depths at the ocean floor
where the mountains rise from the planet's core
there is a tempered mass carefully formed.

The base is the breadth of all history
where the steps climb upon all that has been
ascending steepening difficulties.

And as they climb they extend through time
with ridges along the heightening lines
to where the summits touch each star in the sky.

And with each Herculean feat she achieves
she overcomes every challenge with ease
and draws the world to the tip of her feet.

GARRETT BUHL ROBINSON

She may appear to float feather light
yet with the strength in the wings of her life
she lifts the mountain higher with her flight.

And with devoted labor borne with finesse,
so impossible tasks appear effortless,
she makes lightning strike with her arabesque.

A Lifetime Every Day

DANCER
& ENSEMBLE OF DANCERS

>Every day in our lives we strive
>>to reach this stage
>and this rigorous routine
>>is our life every day.

>We live our lives inside
>>the studio's space
>and fill this empty corridor
>>with elegant grace.

>We follow the steps of others
>>but we must find our own paths
>making the roles our own
>>in the confines we are cast.

>Each day begins with lessons
>>we learned as children
>standing at the barre
>>stretching and extending.

>Then hour upon hour
>>we continue to build
>and with the whet stone of class
>>we keen the edge of our skills.

With comportment and poise
  we stand statue smooth
and from this solid base
  we may fluently move.

We must be carefully composed
  before we can be free.
It is a heavy labor
  to achieve this liberty.

Then in the evening we may
  perform on the stage,
in the course of the hours we live
  a lifetime every day.

With every fiber of our lives
  and all that we do,
all that we are we leave
  on the stage for you.

We can sharpen our focus
  to the point of a pin
then span the whole world
  to draw everyone in.

And all the abundance we offer
  of passion and grace,
we miraculously draw
  from the vacancy of space.

BEAUTY BEYOND REASON

We can float in a moment,
   touch the floor with ease.
We can rise through the air
   and dance on the breeze.

We only show the beauty
   and hide the difficulties,
we live saintly lives, suffering
   to set others free.

We bound over walls
   and open the gates
for the rush of the music
   in the movement we make.

There are passages of life
   and countless destinations
but every step we take
   is a deliberate statement.

Life is not described
   in what we say,
the greatest explanation
   is living this way.

Through what is accomplished
   and all we give
the meaning of our lives
   is the way we live.

And since we were children
  and every single day,
we start with empty space
  and fill it with beauty and grace.

To Touch Eternity

DANCER
& ENSEMBLE OF DANCERS

> There are the moments of our life
>   when everything intersects,
> where every wonder coincides
>   in every single aspect.
>
> All the dancers rush together
>   to rise in a surge
> and all our strength is combined
>   to perfectly converge.
>
> Then we scatter like sparks
>   from the stone of our grind,
> wheels of our own worlds
>   corresponding in time.
>
> We weave our lives together
>   through the warp and weft,
> span the loam of the stage
>   with our intricate steps.
>
> We must learn the roles
>   and move through memory,
> plunging through rivers of music
>   in the dancer's ecstasy.

GARRETT BUHL ROBINSON

Every moment is unique
   with every endeavor.
Time does not repeat,
   every instant is forever.

The audience leaps to their feet
   and stands in awe
and we rise into the sky
   on their thunderous applause.

But when the performance is past
   and the curtain drops,
in the haunting stillness
   there is a sense of loss.

We sacrifice our youth,
   with a thousand lives we would do the same,
even though all our passion
   is only repaid with pain.

We spend a lifetime of struggle
   for the impossible feat
to touch a single moment
   of eternity.

Answer

POET

> There are the essentials of life
> and the demands of the people
> but when one asks who can advise
> the directions of our lives
> through the engagements of our times
> I have a single reply –
>   The answer is the dancers.
>
> With every venture we are told
> there are the critics who will scold
> and try to herd us into folds.
> How can we break the mold
> and live lives that are bold
> and not step on each other's toes –
>   The answer is the dancers.
>
> Often you'll hear people complain
> in a frightful state of dismay
> how we can't properly engage
> in civil and righteous ways
> on the world's far spanning stage.
> I have only one thing to say –
>   The answer is the dancers.

When we wonder on our paths
and the attitudes we all have
so we may fulfill every scene
in every single act
so our lives may interact
without a devastating crash –
   The answer is the dancers.

When we question what can be
to fulfill our capacity
and satisfy the diverse needs
for the good of posterity
so we can live in harmony
in a fluid society –
   The answer is the dancers.

As they move beautifully
it is a marvel to see,
a practice that does not preach
while leading us to release
in the endless ways to be.
To truly learn how to be free –
   The answer is the dancers.

Some Say

DANCER
& ENSEMBLE OF DANCERS

>Some say the dance is contrived –
>   we only follow the steps,
>obeying the directions
>   we are forced to accept.
>
>Some may say we perform
>   only what we are told
>but we all play parts in our lives
>   and perform different roles.
>
>Some say one person must lead
>   and others fall into place,
>the scenes are all arranged
>   and the music sets the pace.
>
>We all have obligated parts,
>   yet the matters of fact
>is what we can make of ourselves
>   in the roles we are cast.
>
>To reach the soaring heights
>   the climb is intense
>and we must work for years
>   to earn one evening's lift.

Nothing is ever for certain,
   there's no guarantee,
we may work our whole lives
   for only misery.

Some may think we are fools
   struggling through agony,
sacrificing decades for one
   fleeting chance to be free.

Have we wasted our whole lives
   for a frivolous show?
If we never give up
   then at least we will know.

And even if we fail
   and suffer hardships and grief,
at least we'll have that certainty,
   that's more than most people achieve.

But there is nothing that compares
   with an opening night
when the audience's applause
   sends us soaring into flight.

And on the rare occasions
   in the theater's lights
we have a heavenly chance
   to touch numberless lives.

BEAUTY BEYOND REASON

Our work is inspiration
  in all we achieve
and through our personal struggles
  we set everyone free.

Relying on Rivals, Competing against Friends
– for MF

DANCER
& ENSEMBLE OF DANCERS

>The pace is relentless
>   all of the time,
>one tiny slip
>   and you're left behind.
>
>And when you're out
>   they'll send you home
>to dance in the darkness
>   and all alone.
>
>There are veterans who will mock you
>   in the hauteur of renown,
>say you'll never reach their level
>   while they try to hold you down.
>
>And if you break free
>   they might push you to the edge
>then all gather to laugh
>   while you tumble off the ledge.
>
>Everyone wants to have friends
>   but they come at a cost,
>knowing those bonds are precious
>   and in an instant can be lost.

BEAUTY BEYOND REASON

We all hope to be accepted
   but no one can tell
we're at the center of the world
   yet all by ourselves.

We have a tireless ambition
   to perfect our art,
yet it's a lonely achievement
   when we set ourselves apart.

We tread on treacherous steps
   no one would recommend,
relying on our rivals
   and competing against friends.

Then domineering coaches
   will visit from afar
and demand we be what they think
   and not who we are.

Then we struggle for a part
   to see it given away
to some others who are clueless
   about the money their parents gave.

But there's no sense in complaining.
   We've all slogged up that hill.
"This isn't about art honey,
   this is about paying the bills!"

We are all on a caravan
   living our gypsy lives,
and all together we laugh,
   and all together we cry.

The Noble Part

DANCER
& ENSEMBLE OF DANCERS

>All our life we take lessons
>   and every day we are taught
>how to take something this hard
>   and make it supple and soft.
>
>We all make compromises
>   to clear each other's way
>but we can't stifle our passion
>   when we perform on the stage.
>
>Ever step has a purpose
>   while everyone moves.
>You can't just know your own part,
>   but all the other parts too.
>
>Life is fraught with frustration,
>   an endless source of dismay,
>but to make it look easy
>   is the gift of ballet.
>
>In this relentless rigor
>   solving complexity,
>we take the most baffling steps
>   and make them fluent and free.

We could frazzle computers
   with impossible math
to arrange the overlapping
   of our intricate paths.

And when we make our leaps
   we can't hesitate,
we must trust that the others
   are all in their place.

We'll dive without a flinch
   to fall in an embrace,
we dance in trust and love
   as much as time and space.

It's the map of memory
   astoundingly precise
with the counts of our hearts
   and the measures of our minds.

And even if it looks gentle,
   as sweet as a song,
it's like singing an opera
   while running a marathon.

And pursuing the work
   so every fiber is strained,
we reveal the beauty
   while we conceal the pain.

We may be secretly wincing
   while we glide on the floor,
yet we withhold all our anguish
   and reveal only joy.

We all suffer through hardships,
   we all struggle through life,
the dancers endure the worst
   and only offer delight.

It is the comportment of character
   that is carefully refined
reminding the audience
   of the dignity of our lives.

Absolutely Endless

DANCER
& ENSEMBLE OF DANCERS

    Some say understanding
      is the way we think
    when the notions of our thoughts
      and the world agree.

    But there is more to our lives
      then just our thinking
    and we are processing our feelings
      through the whole life we are living.

    It is a silly notion
      to divide the body and mind.
    Our whole body is a thought.
      We think with our whole life.

    While the mind sorts sensations
      of our experience,
    the arrangements of our lives
      is our mind's embodiment.

    We feel the presence of others
      as we encounter them
    and they communicate with us
      through what their minds intend.

We are welcomed into their worlds
   through what they reveal
and are confused with the blocks
   of what they conceal.

And often upon the blocks
   that are exposed
we project our own conclusions
   from what we presume to know.

So much of what we are
   is what others expect
and what we cherish of ourselves
   others often reject.

How can we be confined
   to what other's misconceive?
Our evidence is our life
   too often misperceived.

The completeness of our lives
   is achieved mutually,
everyone all together
   is our reality.

And this intricate world
   of what we are
is best illustrated
   in the performing arts.

Every single production
  is a collaboration
between artist and audience
  for every presentation.

Then in the performance hall
  through reflective attention
the understanding achieved
  is the greatest creation.

The art is the audience
  in how they think and feel.
The work is the artists
  and their talents and skills.

The complete work of art
  is not just the performance.
The complete work of art is the
  collective experience.

The changing shapes of our minds
  arrange our whole lives
and our lives depend on how
  the arrangements combine.

What is witnessed on the stage
  is a conception of the mind,
developed and refined
  through an entire lifetime.

Every part is imbued
  with each personality
as the audience and dancers
  combine elaborately.

There are constant adjustments
  every single night
and a myriad of perspectives
  of each individual life.

When considering all the factors
  of every performance,
the meaning of every expression
  is absolutely endless.

GARRETT BUHL ROBINSON

Partnering the Heart
– for LL

DANCER
& ENSEMBLE OF DANCERS

       More than breaking your heart,
       it can tear you apart,
       there is a great frustration
          and a tormenting trouble
       to be partnered with one
          but in love with another.

       We draw attention to the stage
       to touch lives far away,
       but often what crowds around us
          is not what we expect,
       we get so much attention,
          but so little respect.

       And when the mobs pile around
       and trample us down,
       we may search through the crowd
          hoping to see,
       but through the shoves and shouts
          love is hassled to leave.

       The true one knows every step,
       each moment is a caress.

BEAUTY BEYOND REASON

We are perfect complements
   building each other up,
firm with the lifts
   yet tender to touch.

Every time we are together
we feel we're made for each other,
all we are combines
   as our hearts coincide
to circulate all we love
   throughout both of our lives.

Even apart from each other
we are drawn closer together.
What may lack in presence
   our devotion's persistence
extends our love
   to span any distance.

We have our own careers
we have worked on for years
but if our duties are different
   as they diverge
they broaden our life
   in each enriching return.

Together is our home.
The life we live is one.
And all that we share

is all that we are
and when we embrace we have
   all we want in our arms.

There are conventional parts,
then the partnering of the heart.
Our first love is dance
   but we must make a stand
when a woman loves a woman
   and a man loves a man.

More than breaking your heart,
it can tear you apart,
there is a great frustration
   and a tormenting trouble
when you're partnered with one
   but in love with another.

Epilogue

I told her – You have given me the most magnificent idea for a book.

She simply looked at me in a way only a dancer can, as if the entire universe suddenly stopped around her, and she said – Then write it.

And I did.

Pas Seul

Serenade
    — for George Balanchine

Mr. B. sits at the tip of the wing,
he knows the piece, he knows what to expect,
there is always the inevitable misstep,
his interest now is watching the audience.
Behind the curtain, he knows the routine,
choice dancers of the corps, the trembling breath,
then the salve of the soothing release
and from this calm the strings begin to sing.
With an ethereal blue the curtain lifts
and the dancers – standing, enchanting,
after years reaching for the impossible –
touch the divine with their fingertips.
Then a whispered phrase as smooth as a pearl,
"Now, my dears, you may dance before the world."

Pas Seul
    — for the Oregon Ballet Theatre

Clumsily we depict grace as a gift
that nature has flippantly bestowed
upon them but down the arduous road,
enclosed by the recital curtain's rift,
exhausting strains to lithe the tensing stiff
bodies aching with laborious loads
refresh the streams where elegance flows
and spring to life ballet's delightful lift.

How oblivious we are to the years
of agonizing struggles to perfect
what is casually watched from the tiers.
Only earnest attention can respect
how often the streams would dry if not for tears
to buoy the burden of graceful effect.

Exchanging Gifts
   — for Janice Garrett and Dancers

Every moment is no more than itself
extending into the enveloping
of everything else. Wrapping around one
another, lacing awareness throughout
interaction, dancers wove wings of silk
and lifted me to where the constellations
scattered as the stone robes of convention
dismantled in an expanding whirl of stars.
Your correspondence of arrangements is
often not in motion but of moving
the universe around your crystal stillness.
Your work is not puppetry, pantomime
or music embodied in instruments.
Your work is life – literally divine.

The Way You Say

>Every statement has the potential for poetry
>as all movement has the potential for dance.

Dancer, your voice is the wind
you make in your movement.
Your song is your whole being
as your whole being is singing.

Dashing past, your gust is a wake
unfolding over the shore
as you arch into the open
to draw me into your quiet deep.

The pulse of your turn twirls
at the edge of uncertainty,
spinning the mystic distance
into the thread of your passage.

I have felt the pressure nudge
as you slip through the creases of space,
wing smooth, absent of turbulence,
a slice through air in your endless lift.

I have seen your floating fingertips,
each touch sending waves lapping
softer than water as you play
space – your instrument.

But what leaves me breathless
is the sight of you standing still,
statuesque magnificence,
and around you – the air trembles.

Poured from a Performance

When I watch you dance upon the stage
I feel pressed up against the back wall
and although you may appear a mile away
your touch is an irresistible draw.
When you turn, the whole world spins
and stars trace perfect circles over your head
while your delicate steps send ripples
that caress the countless lives you impress.
Then in an instant I feel a sudden shock
as if an arrow plunged through my heart,
but instead of mortally bleeding
my entire life is filled with sweetness
as cupid's bow floats with a humming string
and the shivering river of music leaves me quivering.

Dancing Elms

Legend says Orpheus sang and played
with such beauty, the trees
would pull their roots from the ground
and dance.

Once, while he strolled through the woods,
strumming the strings of his harp,
filling the air with melodious
poetry,

the elms began to sway,
undulating their outstretching
limbs in the fluent
music.

Then for some reason unknown,
perhaps hearing Eurydice
pleading, heartbroken and alone,
he stopped

and in the most elegant, flowing pose,
all the trees froze.

Agape

Yesterday I attended a reading
where poets bewailed the world
for not being like it used to be.

Then I heard others recite lines
rebuking the world for not giving
them all that they want.

Then I watched myself compose
a brief piece where I complained
about other people complaining.

In the evening, I moped down the street
to visit a local theater and find a seat
before a performance.

Dancer, I know why I love you.
You never tell me what to think.
You show me how to live.

Note

Serenade, Pas Seul, Exchanging Gifts, The Way You Say and Dancing Elms have been previously published.

Acknowledgements

B.T. Shaw, Oliver Buck, Nina Liebman, Ken Wein, Dennis Brown, Jesse Waters, The Actors Fund and Breaking Ground New York City

Garrett Buhl Robinson was born in Alabama in 1971. He began composing verse at 16 years of age when his sister gave him his first book of poetry: Shakespeare's Sonnets. In 1992, he jumped on a coal train and left his home town. He has been wandering around the United States ever since while studying intensely and writing prolifically. In 2015, he made his Off-Broadway debut performing his solo musical: *Letters to Zoey*.